T0146894

I Gotta Tell Ya

You Got This, Kid

WRITTEN BY REBECCA ZADEGAN

ILLUSTRATED BY RICHARD SCOTT

BALBOA.PRESS

A DIVISION OF HAY HOUSE

Balboa Press books may be ordered through booksellers or by contacting:

Balboa Press
A Division of Hay House
1663 Liberty Drive
Bloomington, IN 47403
www.balboapress.com.au
1 (877) 407-4847

Print information available on the last page.

ISBN: 978-1-5043-2108-2 (sc)
ISBN: 978-1-5043-2109-9 (e)

Balboa Press rev. date: 05/05/2020

Contents

"If there is light in the soul, there will be beauty in the person. If there is beauty in the person, there will be harmony in the house. If there is harmony in the house, there will be order in the nation. If there is order in the nation, there will be peace in the world."

Dedication

This book is dedicated to my son.

You teach me every day to be intentional in every moment. I waited lifetimes for you, Kid. It's so nice to finally see your eyes.

To all the children that I have come to know.
Thank you for sharing your magic with me.

May you always choose your wand.
May you always know your power.

xoxo

Your Wand

Every kid has a wand, regardless of the shape or size.
This wand is how you create your magic. No one else can make your wand work.
It only knows you.
It can help you when you feel stuck. It can help you when you feel sad.
You can move things and you can move people. But most importantly,
you can change the energy to whatever you want it to be.
Your wand is your best toy. You will know what to do with it because only YOU know
how to work it. Every wand works differently because every person is different.
You have the power to do amazing and magical things.
You can create anything you like. Change anything you need.
Every minute. Every day. Wherever you are.
If you can't change the feeling, colour it in, until the feeling changes.
If you don't feel safe, create a bubble around you.
If you want the green dragon, but you got the red,
wave your wand. Change the colour.
You are magical, kid.
Your wand is an extension of you. You are the boss, not the wand. Care
for it. Treat it gently. Stay connected to it. It is always with you.

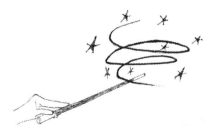

How do I know?
Because I have seen you use it.

The Big Ones

I know when you came out of my tummy, into this reality, there is so
much of it that didn't make sense. There is so much of it that doesn't feel
light, fun or joyful. In fact, it feels painful, scary and hard. And it is.
But it doesn't need to be, kid. And you know a better way.
You see, the big ones, we call ourselves adults, are doing the best we can with
what we have. But the problem is, we have forgotten that we have wands too.
There are things we do every day we should be doing every year.
There are things we do every year we should be doing every day.
We have all jumped on a little rat wheel and are too busy
watching our feet to see the other rides in the park.
And there are other rides in the park. Because I've ridden them.
And those rides are more peaceful. More playful. More fun.
Us big ones can't look up or we'll fall. So we just keep running.
Don't get on the wheel, kid.
Us big ones have forgotten we have the ability to choose something new.

How do I know?
Because to get somewhere you've never been, you have to
be prepared to do something you've never done.
And we haven't done it yet.

The Park

There are so many rides in the park.
We all get to choose which one we ride.

Some will get on a ride and complain, and vomit, and
scream. But they won't get off the ride.
It's not your job to press the stop button. It's theirs.

Some rides will make you laugh, and some will make you scream.
You choose which slot to put your coin.

If you choose the fast and crazy ride, you'll get a fast and crazy day.
Choose your ride. Choose your day.

How do I know?
Because I've chosen the ride that made me vomit,
and it was not a good day.

Words

Every word you speak carries an energy.

Just like in BFG (our favourite movie!) when you see the dreams and nightmares

in the jars, bouncing around, with all sorts of colours and speeds.

Words are exactly the same.

Us humans can say the most hurtful things.

When someone is saying something hurtful, use your wand and put a bell-shaped

jar over them so you can't hear them. You know those times when someone

speaks to you in a way that feels heavy or hurts your heart? Those times.

Let their words bounce off the little jar and land right back at

their feet where they can choose what to do with them.

You can choose what words you let out of your mouth. Every time.

Speak from that place inside of you that feels light and playful and true.

Speak with the knowing that those words will land back at your feet one day.

Speak like you are speaking to yourself, in every moment.

Because you are.

V	O	L	E	S	J	J
T	Q	O	A	R	U	L
C	A	V	N	U	D	U
E	K	I	N	D	G	F
P	M	N	T	E	I	T
S	D	G	O	Z	N	R
E	M	R	P	I	G	U
R	L	S	E	R	R	H
O	M	A	G	I	C	O

Kind ☐   Rude ☐

Loving ☐ Hurtful ☐

Respect ☐ Judging ☐

How do I know?
Because when I speak to you,
I feel the energy in me.

The Dark Side

We all know the feeling of the darkness.
Some of us feel lonely, scared or sad in that room. Sometimes it makes
you feel like you're in the wrong playground, country or planet.
Have you got your wand? Does it need a service or some attention?
Put every little piece of your big dark room into a jar and shake it.
Shake it until the light breaks through. Darkness is just
another colour. And colours can be changed.
Wash your eyeballs in bubbles and put them back in.
Sometimes you'll sit in that dark room for longer, and that's
okay, but don't forget you are holding your wand.
Create something. Open a door. Replace the battery in the torch.
Do whatever it is you need to do to move. Lift your head up a bit.
Just move. Take one step. Shake your arms. You got this, Kid.
There are scary things. There are dark things. But then there's You. Have you
met You? Go and look in the mirror and look at that little dark circle in your
eye. Stare at that. For 3 minutes. Now tell me, what are you still afraid of?
Yes, you will fall one day. But you will get up. Yes, you will cry. But you will then laugh.
Yes, you will hurt. But you will then heal. Yes, you will lose. But you have already won.
Why? Because you have You. Your wand has You. And you, kid, are Magic in Motion.

How do I know?
Because I've seen your moves, baby. And you rock my world.

The Window

Everywhere there are windows.

Wherever you look, it will be through a window.
You can choose which one.
The round one. The square one. The arch one. The diamond one.

All will show you something different.

If you don't like what you see, change your window.
Whichever shape you look through, you will see only from that shape.

And remember, you have the magic to build a new shape.

How do I know?
Because you built one for me.

The Wonky Path

Some of us big ones think the path we have paved is the only path.
We think that there are different signs and different things to look
at, but we are convinced that the path is the only path.
Look to the left, kid.
There is a sneaky little alley that only you know about. And it goes at your
speed, with only your wheels and has as many stops as you need.
It is new and it has not yet had footprints left there.
When you walk on that path, your feet are stable, your
chin is up and your arms are swinging.
Some of us big ones think that your path will be the long way, the hard
way, the wrong way. Just wave, smile and continue walking.
If you start to feel like you are in the wrong shoes, seeing out the wrong window,
have the wrong key to every door.... pick up your wand and get back on your path.
We can stay on our own paths and chat over the bushes.
You will know when you have moved from your path.

How do I know?
Because you don't smile on the wonky path,
you will only smile when you make your own tracks.

The Map

Us big ones seem to think that the map is the only map.
But the funny thing about the map, is the map is not even required.
We have signs and street names and speed limits.
We have green lights and red lights and lines. We have roads.
We have roads to schools, jobs, marriages, money bags, boats, cars,
animals, clothes and shops and restaurants and all sort of things.
Just remember us big ones can't always see what you see.
And that doesn't mean those things aren't there.
You don't have to keep giving us different glasses to see what you see, you can just
turn our chairs around and let us see what we can with the glasses that we have.
Draw your own map.
You choose your vehicle. You choose the speed.
You choose the road. You choose the need.

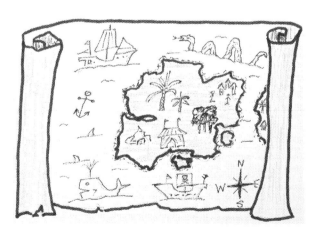

How do I know?
Because this world doesn't know your map yet.
And the map we have now is too small for your kind of magic, kid.

The Ladder

You must remember that sometimes you will feel like you can't speak, you aren't being heard and that you are misunderstood. Or you'll be in the dark room for too long. Or you'll be so mad and angry that you feel stuck in it. You may feel like someone else is pulling you along, dragging you away, lifting you up or pushing you down. You will feel like you're a toothless dragon – you will know what is possible and you will know your power, but you'll feel too far from it.

Go to the Ladder.
Every step you take up this ladder your body gets lighter, your backpack gets smaller, your darkness gets brighter and your smile gets wider. By the time you reach the top of the ladder you will be wide-open mouthed, laughing and feeling light again. You will know when you need this ladder, because your mouth will be closed, your lips will feel heavy, your eyes will be heavy, your heart will hurt, your fists will be closed and your words will feel stuck.

How do I know?
Because you led me to that ladder.

The River

When you are creating your footprints, you will know when
you get off your path, because you'll start to feel like you're in
a boat, and can't stop it, turn it, anchor it or control it.
You're trying so hard to get to the shore, but you can't. You
will be paddling like mad, and the trip will be hard.
Pull your oars in, kid.
The river will take you to the path.

Stop fighting the current, paddling upstream, looking
for the shore, searching for your path.

Pull them in and enjoy the ride.
Watch for things that make you smile and light you up with joy.
You are safe, and exactly where you are meant to be.
You can never get lost. Just pull your oars in.

How do I know?
Because a river can never flow the wrong way.

Fuel

Your body is the most powerful machine you will ever know.

It has powers even scientists don't know about yet.

Your body will hold you strong and protect your spirit

and your wand for as long as you need it to.

It's like an engine, so fuel it wisely.

You don't put diesel in an unleaded only tank. Learn about your tank.

If you let the doors rust off, you'll fall out.

If the windows are dirty, clean them. If you can't see, you'll crash.

This is the same for your thoughts.

Clean your negative thoughts, or you will crash.

This is the same for your food.

Choose your foods, or you will clog the pipe.

The path you choose won't matter if you have no vehicle to travel in.

Your magic is free and flowing when your engine is free and flowing.

Support it. Service it. Fuel it. Pump up the tyres. Fill the water.

Give it a clean out. Regularly.

And it matters, you know, what you put into it.

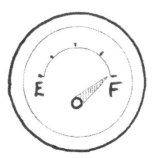

How do I know?
Because I've had a clogged pipe, and it makes the race harder.

The Wave

Stand by the ocean and watch the waves come in and then go out.
That is what happens here too.
You will have times when you are just bobbing on top of the water, waiting
for the next good wave. You'll learn how to pick the good ones.
You will have times when you have to paddle like mad to get out
of the white water. You'll learn when to dive under or over.
You will have times when you are cruising on the greatest wave, and everybody
cheers. You'll learn that these are often after a great deal of paddling, or waiting....
You will have times when you fall, and everybody sees. You'll learn
that you can always get back up and paddle out again.
But remember, your wave will always come. You will get your moment.
So enjoy the paddle out. Enjoy sitting on the board, waiting.

How do I know?
Because I've had my moment.
And I've learnt to paddle hard and to wait for my wave.

The Tree

Some people in this world are not kind. And some are.
You will know the difference because your wand will flicker when
something or someone doesn't match your magic.

When you meet Unkindness, you will know because you
will find some unkindness within yourself.

When we don't see the Unkindness Tree, the roots are no longer in us.
When we don't see the Anger Tree, the roots are no longer in us.

You will always see what is rooted within you.
You have a choice to shake the Kindness Tree, or the Unkindness Tree.
And remember, whatever tree you shake the leaves will fall on you too.

How do I know?
Because I've stood under both trees,
and one makes me feel a lot better than the other.

Boats

We can point our boats in whatever direction we choose,
but if we don't put the sail up, we won't move.
Birds can fly into it and tear it.
People can steal it straight from your boat.
Fix the sail. Buy another one. Keep your boat moving.
There will be other boats around you. All facing different
directions. Some with sails. Some without. Some capsizing.
Some anchored. Some with one person. Some with four.

Stay in your own boat, kid.

You have big dreams and wide-open shores ready and waiting for you.
Ready and waiting for your magic to be heard, felt and seen.

Put the sail up.
And if your boat stops moving, look up. It's just a sail needing to be fixed.

How do I know?
Because I know boats, kid.

Bandaids

Some things are gonna hurt. I can't change that for you.

I can give you bandaids and I can wash off the dirt.

But ultimately it is your body that will heal the wound.

Sometimes there are pain waves you are just going to have to ride, Kid. I

can join you on the wave, but you have to stand on your own board.

And you can.

You have a golden ball inside of you that will tell you what to do.

You will know.

That ball will bounce around inside your body, bathing you with golden light

and heal everything that needs to be healed. It will give you the courage to

ride the waves. It will give you the strength to mend any kind of wound.

That golden ball knows all the twists and turns in

your body and will never miss a corner.

That golden ball is yours and can be trusted.

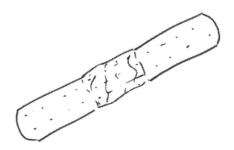

How do I know?
Because I have my own golden ball and it's never been wrong.

The Garden Hose

There will be times when people say or do things that
melt you and make you feel amazing.
It will give you the best and most magical feeling inside. Remember it and
put your hands up to the big sky and ask for MORE! MORE! MORE!
You can get this feeling from so many people and so many places.
Not just one. They are scattered all through your
life like the stars in the sky above you.
They will make you feel good. Without even really trying.
They'll be there to remind you when you start to get a bit tough on yourself.
They'll be there to make you feel safe. Heard. Valued. And loved.

Things change and people change.
Friendships are like gardens. If you don't water them, they'll die.
Put the effort into your friends. And they'll put the effort into you.
And remember who you are when you make your friends.
You are gold. You are magical. You are love itself.
But remember, you need to water your own garden first. If
you don't, you'll have no colour to share or to give.

How do I know?
Because I spent a long time watering everyone else's garden.
Until I realised that I had forgotten to water mine.

The Key

Deep inside of you there is a little room. A little room that knows good from bad.
The world is full of people.
All who want different things. Say different things. Wear different things.
That little room inside of you will know when
something is inside of it that shouldn't be.
And some people will tell you that you need to keep it in there.
Some people will tell you that if you open the room and tell someone what's
in it, that you'll get in to trouble or that you'll cause someone pain.
The thing with the room is, that only you have the key.
You get to decide what stays in it, and what comes out of it.
Remember though, anything that isn't matching your magic will feel yuck.
All you need to do is get the little key hanging on the little
wall, next to the little door, for your little room.
And let it out.
Find someone you trust and open the room.
Stories and memories can only cause you pain, feel yuck and fill your
little room if you don't open the door every now and then.
And no one else gets to choose when you get to open the door. Only you do.
You have the key. It is your door. It is your room.

How do I know?
I kept mine shut for too long and I started to feel sick.

Blankets

There is goodness everywhere. There is love everywhere.

You'll know it when you have it because you'll feel warm
and fuzzy and safe and happy and full.
There is also the other stuff. And you will know that too, because
you will not feel warm and fuzzy and safe and happy and full.
You are a big, beautiful blanket of goodness and adventure and fun
and peace and love – all wrapped up as the most perfect gift.
You have so much magic in your blanket it will probably scare people
when you open it up. People are often scared of what they don't
know or recognise. But don't let that stop you opening it.

Open your blanket, kid.
The world needs it.

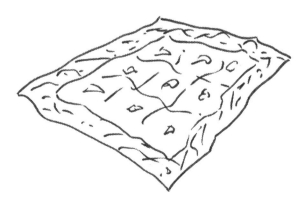

How do I know?
Because you've wrapped me in it and it's one of my favourite places to be.

The Chessboard

You are living in a world that is no different to a chessboard.
There are many different pieces on the board, all moving
in different directions with different abilities.
Some move one square, others ten. Some move sideways, others forward.
If you don't learn the rules of the board, you will start:

Reacting - not creating.
Blaming - not owning.
Pointing - not accepting.
Fearing - not trusting.
Judging – not allowing.
Resisting – not releasing.

How do I know?
Because I'm on the same board, and the rules are universal.

Your Lane

You are only responsible for You.
You, and you alone.
You can change your togs, your goggles, your speed and where you are in the race.
But stay in your lane. If you get into someone else's
lane, someone is going to get kicked, kid.

If you take responsibility for your happiness, you will
have a wonderful, happy and magical life.
If you hand the responsibility over to someone else, it will be
impossible for you to live a wonderful, happy and magical life.

If you don't like what you have or what you do – change it.
And if you are happy, everyone and everything around will be too.

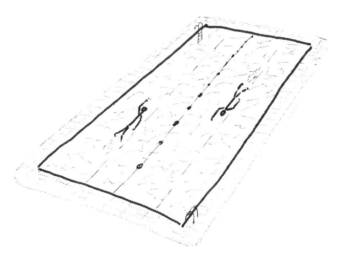

How do I know?
Because when I feel happy, I see more happy people.

Your Tingle

You know, your body is like a compass to goodness. It will vibrate, or tingle or tighten in a spot when it is telling you that something doesn't match your magic.

This might mean that someone or something around you isn't good for you. Trust the tingle. It is trying to communicate with you. You might be going to do something you know is going to hurt someone. Your tingle will jingle. You might be saying something that isn't true. Your tingle will jingle. You might be about to get in a car with a stranger. Your tingle will jingle.

No one else can hear your tingle because their tingle will jingle differently. Trust your own.

How do I know?
Because your tingle was created to guide and protect you.

You

There will be days when you trip, drop your wand or sink the boat.
Let me remind you of Who You Are for the days you will forget.
You are powerful. You are magical.
You are beautiful. And you are Free.

You are a magnificent human being, living in a world of great possibility.
You are not broken. You are not alone.
We are all with you. Backing you. Whispering in your ear.
You got this, kid.

And you are exactly where you are meant to be.

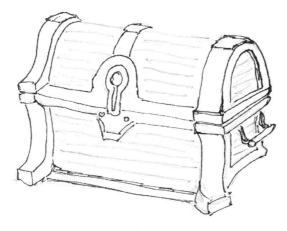

How do I know?
Because you're there.

My Hot Tips

Find something to make you smile every day. No matter what.

What you do to yourself, you do to others. What you do to others, you do to yourself.

Be responsible for your words and your actions – all of them.

Build trust with your actions and lead by example. Be first to say sorry.

Clean up if you make a mess. On the table, or in someone's life.

Let yourself really love - or you deprive the world of You.

Keep connected - to yourself, to your Earth and to your world.

Do something every day to keep the connection.

Reach out - if you need help, ask for it. No one can do it alone.

Rock out to your favourite music regularly. Loud and loose baby!

We are all choosing what we experience, whether we want to believe it or not.

"Stop trying to fit in, when you were born to stand out"

Surround yourself by people and things that make you happy.

You become like them, and they become like you.

Be responsible for your own education of life. A belief

is only a belief if people believe in it.

Question everything. Follow your heart. Beat to your own drum.

Know that every new beginning comes from some other beginning's end.

All is well.

Now go be magical, kid. Because you are.

Acknowledgements

This book is inspired from our favourite song (that we sing regularly like a prayer, at full volume, in our lounge room with our hands in the air and smiles on our faces...) *'Love My Life'*, by Robbie Williams.

And

One day I heard Reese Witherspoon say something like *'I wanted to leave Hollywood in a better state than I found it."* And I realized, we all have that power. Whether it be a family line, a classroom, a community or a country.

They are two of the many artists who seek to create a different possibility for our children, in a world that is off track.

And I respect that.

Thank you to my Mum, who reminds me so gently when I drop my wand. To my Dad, for his incredible gift of illustrating my first book! My bro and his lovely, growing little family, for always being there for me.

Thank you to all the people, places and spaces I have seen and been.

Thank you for music, camping under the stars, my dog, incense, night roadies and romantic comedies.

Thank you for genuine human connection. May every one of you have the courage to provide it and the privilege of experiencing it.

Most of all, thank you to my children – for being the most magical Beings I have ever met.

I love my life. Forever Grateful xoxo

Look out for the second book in the *I Gotta Tell Ya* trilogy:

This One's for You, Mav!

For all of you out there wondering what you've got yourselves into being
alive at such a time in the history of the human race. You are not alone.
You are not broken. You are not misplaced. You are not a freak.
You are Golden. You are Unique. And You are SO required right now.
Here is the story that underpins the little lessons I learnt and shared in the
first book. This is where the rubber hit the road. This is the juice within the
cup. Some things you'd think I was making up. Nope. It all happened.
This is where I found clarity in the chaos.... This is where I found out Who I Really Am.

Printed in the United States
By Bookmasters